PAINT

New & Easy Decorating Library

BETTER HOMES AND GARDENS® BOOKS
Des Moines, Iowa

**New & Easy Decorating Library**
**Better Homes and Gardens® Books  An imprint of Meredith® Books**
**Published for Creative World Enterprises LP, West Chester, Pennsylvania**
**www.1CreativeWorld.com**

**PAINT  Volume 3**
Project Editors: Denise L. Caringer, Linda Hallam
Art Director: Jerry J. Rank
Copy Chief: Catherine Hamrick
Copy and Production Editor: Terri Fredrickson
Contributing Copy Editor: Margaret Smith
Contributing Proofreaders: Kathy Eastman, Colleen Johnson, Gretchen Kauffman
Electronic Production Coordinator: Paula Forest
Editorial and Design Assistants: Kaye Chabot, Mary Lee Gavin, Karen Schirm
Production Director: Douglas M. Johnston
Production Managers: Pam Kvitne, Marjorie J. Schenkelberg

**Meredith® Books**
Editor in Chief: James D. Blume
Design Director: Matt Strelecki
Managing Editor: Gregory H. Kayko

Director, Sales & Marketing, Retail: Michael A. Peterson
Director, Sales & Marketing, Special Markets: Rita McMullen
Director, Sales & Marketing, Home & Garden Center Channel: Ray Wolf
Director, Operations: George A. Susral

Vice President, General Manager: Jamie L. Martin

***Better Homes and Gardens*® Magazine**
Editor in Chief: Jean LemMon
Executive Interior Design Editor: Sandra S. Soria

**Meredith Publishing Group**
President, Publishing Group: Christopher M. Little
Vice President, Consumer Marketing & Development: Hal Oringer

**Meredith Corporation**
Chairman and Chief Executive Officer: William T. Kerr

Chairman of the Executive Committee: E. T. Meredith III

**Creative World Enterprises LP**
Publisher: Richard J. Petrone
Design Consultants to Creative World Enterprises: Coastline Studios, Orlando, Florida

All of us at Better Homes and Gardens® Books are dedicated to providing you with information and ideas to enhance your home. We welcome your comments and suggestions. Write to us at: Better Homes and Gardens Books, Shelter Editorial Department, 1716 Locust St., Des Moines, IA 50309-3023.

If you would like to purchase any of our books, check wherever quality books are sold. Visit our website at bhg.com or bhgbooks.com.

# CONTENTS

## New & Easy Decorating With Paint

Creating a stylish and welcoming home is immensely satisfying, and paint is a quick, budget-friendly way to get there. Live in your house awhile to get used to its eccentricities—the movement of light or a room's odd shape—before making any major color decisions.

Begin with a backdrop. For the cost of a can of paint and the time you spend on a decorative finish, you can enliven a dull room. If you aren't sure where to begin, choose a color from your favorite artwork, or from a fabric or rug you plan

Getting STARTED

to use in the room. Find a paint color that matches or complements. If you prefer, have the exact color custom-mixed at your paint store. Or be bold and enjoy your favorite cool and warm colors combined with a decorative finish, *opposite*.

Discover the colors you prefer to live with. Clip photos from magazines and books. Make notes about room backdrops in furniture stores and showhouses. Look through your own clothes closet for your own likes and dislikes. Keep this information in a folder and take it with you as you shop.

Look at the ever-increasing number of stock colors. With every major paint manufacturer and many designers offering a wealth of choices, it's easier than ever to find stylish colors for your home. Some companies offer color schemes so you can pick wall and trim colors or a whole-house color scheme with ease. Personalize a preselected scheme with a decorative finish, such as a fireplace wall that's sponged or ragged, to play up an architectural feature.

**Set a mood with color.** Are you aware there's a correlation between your mood and the colors that surround you? Colors have an impact on your psyche, so it's important to know a little about each one, and how they affect you, before slathering fire-engine red across every wall in the house, or decking your rooms in sunny yellow or deep forest green. What works in one room may not be the best color solution in another. Reds are cheerful, sometimes dramatic, and work in formal and informal settings. They are popular choices for the dining room as they stimulate lively conversation and appetite. The bedroom is usually given a more soothing color to inspire rest. Cool colors—green, blue, lavender—are favorites. Yellow, peaches, and terra-cotta are warm and romantic, appropriate almost anywhere, and especially appealing in sunrooms and family rooms. Use jewel tones to create luxurious, dramatic intimacy in a living or dining room. Forest greens are masculine; pastels are airy; blues are fresh, clean, wholesome, and obviously cool—pairing well with both yellow and white.

**Not-so-plain geometry.** Solid coats of paint are quick room refreshers, as anyone who has ever tried selling their home knows. It's not the most daring approach to paint, however. Paint invites playfulness and an exploration of your personal artistry. Somewhere between intricate freehand murals and simple rolled-on walls of colors lies a stylish compromise: simple geometric forms such as diamonds and stripes. They add pattern and rhythm without busyness. They look sophisticated, yet do not require sophisticated artistic skills.

# Diamonds & STRIPES

**Paint your floors with flair.** Almost any hard flooring surface can be embellished with paint. In a new house with freshly milled hardwood floors, go easy on the color selections. Neutral cream, taupe, and gray work well. So do many pastels, from soft peach or green to grayed plum, often in two-color combinations. With these subtle hues on your floor, it's easy to redecorate or change your home's color palette.

**Diamonds are a floor's best friend.** The easiest way to paint diamonds is with a stencil. One easy, interesting look involves drawing the diamond pattern onto the floor, then painting every other diamond, leaving the others natural wood.

# DIAMONDS & STRIPES

**Try your hand at furniture painting.** The imperfect lines of this splashy, hand-painted artwork are its source of charm, *below*. The bold colors and cheery designs create a custom chest from a flea market find. Polyurethane protects the piece from the rigors of everyday use. Forget the rules about nursery colors. If you like bright, bold colors, such as turquoise and orange, enjoy them. Balance with white and neutrals to keep from overpowering the room. **Climb the walls.** Don't stop with the furniture. Carry your theme up the walls with bright, broken stripes and a jazzy painted star ceiling border, *opposite*.

## STARS AND STRIPES

■ Before beginning the decorative painting, clean, then paint the walls and ceiling with a quality white flat latex.

■ For painted freehand stripes, measure with a yardstick and carpenter's measuring tape for guidelines. Use a pencil to lightly mark lines, and paint freehand over the lines.

■ Practice freehand stars on scrap particleboard or plywood to perfect the look you like. If you're not pleased with the stars, make a star stencil pattern, then place the stencil on the walls and trace around it with a pencil. Finally, paint between the lines.

# DIAMONDS & STRIPES

**Diamonds dress up dated floors.** Not every wood floor is a candidate to be painted in a diamond pattern. Generally, the newer the floor, the less likely it should be painted. But there's an opposite extreme: the historic or aging house, with wood floors that have not weathered well. Paint may be the solution that saves the floors from replacement. It hides stains, camouflages chips, and draws the eye away from imperfections in the wood and gaps in between boards. The extra-large diamond pattern featured in this living room, *opposite* , makes a dramatic style statement with its scale. It also works well in the homeowner's art studio, *above*. Cream-color paint, not bright white, is in keeping with the home's age.

DIAMONDS & STRIPES

**Serene stripes.** This small bedroom deliberately shies away from bright colors and busy patterns to keep it looking as large as possible. It also needed a floor treatment that wasn't dull and predictable. Elegant, lean stripes painted on the wood stretch subtly across the room like light itself.

# DIAMONDS & STRIPES

**Ask the experts.** Check with your paint store for the best paint for the type and condition of your existing wood floor. Oil-based enamels, *opposite,* are durable for high-traffic areas. Also check the colors of paints formulated for porches and floors.

**Stencil on delicacy with a doily.** To create the floor, *right,* measure and mark the center of the floor with an X. Place a doily—this one is about 10 inches square—on the X, then lay out doilies in a checkerboard around it. Leave a 6½-inch-wide border, or cover the whole room. Mark a grid using a yardstick; note solid-color squares by penciling an X at the centers.

**Prepare and apply stencils.** Lay each doily face down on butcher paper and spray lightly with stencil adhesive spray from a crafts store; dry until tacky or sticky to the touch. Put tacky side down on floor, lay paper over it, and rub firmly with your hand.

Lay out the remaining doilies on the floor.

**Tape off the rug border.** Use ½-inch-wide painter's tape that doesn't allow paint to seep under it and doesn't pull up paint when tape is removed. Lay the first border band around the grid pattern; the middle band is 1 inch beyond that, and the outer band is 4 inches beyond the middle band.

**Start to stencil.** Use a 3-inch-wide foam brush and latex paint. Paint solid squares and the border nearest rows you are painting. While that dries, paint doily-covered squares with foam stenciling tool; blot paint off tool on paper towel and dab paint on stencils with an up-and-down motion until holes are filled in. Paint outer border and allow floor to dry about

an hour before adding a second coat of paint. Carefully remove doilies with a razor blade or a heat gun. When the floor is completely dry, brush on a coat of polyurethane sealer.

**Soak up the praise.** This floor is a conversation piece your family and friends will love—and you deserve the praise. Its whimsical look is perfect for a little girl's room or a covered porch.

Whether your style is subtle or bold, rugged or refined, there's a specialty paint treatment that can update a room—or your entire home—without the expense of wallpaper. (An advantage of paint, besides its lower expense, is its ease—no gluey messes to peel off when you're ready for a decorative change.) Painted wall treatments include everything from stripes and diamonds (see previous chapter) to a variety of textured, stenciled, and faux painted surfaces. Faux painting got off to a fast start in the decorating world in the 1980s—and

# Finishes & MOTIFS

continues to grow in popularity. Its origins, however, are centuries old. Faux marble and faux wood paint, as well as a wide range of other types of faux finishes, decorate the historic palaces of European royalty. One well-known example is The Royal Pavilion at Brighton, England. Some of the decorative paint techniques, such as glazing, sponging, and ragging, are easy for anyone who has ever painted a room. The availability of supplies, such as pretextured paint, special brushes, and other tools, makes it easy to achieve artist-quality results with do-it-yourself skills. The only way to hone your talents with special finishes is to pick your technique and supplies—and begin.

# FINISHES & MOTIFS

**Bisect walls with complementary-color paints.** Complementary colors are those hues opposite one another on the color wheel—and they are instant drama for any room. If you're not sure about a color's complement, consult a color wheel (check with your paint store or book store). This formal entry, *opposite,* teams red and its complement, green, using the chair rail molding as the divider.

## REVIVE WITH PAINT

■ Relate colors. Give your rooms separate personalities, but tie the house together by using a unified, ongoing color scheme.

■ Find a fabric you like or plan to use in your room and pull several colors from it.

■ Tape up paint chips and study them at various times of the day and in the evening.

■ Think practically. You wouldn't want a cool blue in a north-facing room, particularly if you live in a cold climate. Hot reds and pinks may overheat a south-facing room. Semigloss, rather than flat finishes, are more durable in high-use spaces.

**Go for bold.** The degree of boldness is up to you. This homeowner's art collection, *above,* already packs a colorful punch. So the thinking is, accentuate the lively mix of styles and frames with jazzy, painted-on color on the walls. To keep the room from appearing too loud and busy, the wall colors were chosen from colors already present in the vintage art. Warm and cool, the coral and green balance each other. When painting walls in different colors, choose colors of the same intensity, rather than a pale tint and saturated color, for pleasing visual balance.

# FINISHES & MOTIFS

**Create an Old World ambience.** Whether your home is two centuries or two years old, you can create a moody, Old World feel with little more than paint on the walls. Applying a paled-down shade of intense color like the terra-cotta in this breakfast room, *opposite*, and adding a second darker shade of the hue, then sponging or ragging the two, creates a mottled, aged look. The lighter moldings and ceiling add high-drama contrast.

**Accentuate with accessories.** The rich, burnished, almost leather look of these walls, *below*, demands decorative accessories to enhance the rugged country European effect. Architectural remnants that have weathered with time are ideal complements. These fancy turned corbels become functional caddies for shelves. In their original condition, they continue the idea of a venerable Tuscan villa. Bright pottery furthers the effect.

**Contrast niches with different paint colors.** If your home features architectural niches, make the most of those assets by calling them to everyone's attention with vividly contrasting paint. The two niches in this hallway, *above,* not only feature a departure from the hallway's ragged rich terra-cotta wall color, they each bear unique paint work. One features a bright periwinkle uniformly applied, and the other is painted with a paler diamond pattern. The result: an arresting focal point.

**Sweet dreams under a star-glazed sky.** Ordinary wall paint creates a flat surface to absorb or reflect light—and, either way, the wall always ends up looking flat. Glaze, however, brings depth to walls, *opposite*. Each coat allows the colors underneath to filter through, adding drama and capturing the play of light. To add texture, sponge, comb, grain, stipple, or rag the still-wet surface. A topping of shiny gold stars makes a sparkling-fine finish.

**Good preparation is important.** Even more so than regular paint, glaze highlights any defects in the wall surface. Don't think you can get by with less preparation by doing a mottled finish; that makes defects more apparent. Patch cracks with caulk, then sand, *above left.*

**Apply the base coat.** Paint the walls and ceiling as you would in a typical project. Here, a dark base coat is applied. The project will go more smoothly if you use a quality enamel for a smooth base coat.

**Gather together all the glazing equipment.** You need a can of tinted glaze, roller and roller pan, large paintbrush, small paintbrush, natural sponge, and several rags for wiping up accidental spills.

**Apply glaze coat and sponge the ceiling.** With all tools ready to go, the magic begins when the first glaze coat is applied. On the ceiling, a tinting glaze in a natural color is applied, then colorants of white titanium, halo blue, and violet from an art store are added to get the desired

chalky hue, *above right.*

**Glaze and pattern the walls.** The next phase involves applying the same glaze but a slightly different tint (less purple, more white) for a lighter look.

**Paint trim and add decorative touches.** After the trim is painted, do any needed touch-up. Here, decorating the ceiling with three sizes of stenciled gold stars completes the one-of-a-kind project. A natural-colored glaze tinted with rich gold powder gives the trim and stars their glow.

**Clean color.** Rooms don't have to be all-white to look breezy and clean, as this multi-color painted bedroom proves, *opposite*. The key to the crisp look lies in keeping the color contrast minimal—the walls' blue, blue-green, and green are all next-door neighbors on the color wheel. The painted white floor and white moldings are the next most important factor in achieving just the right, summery airiness.

**Loving the single life.** Who says monochromatic (single-color) rooms have to be boring? This master bedroom and bath employs some tricks with tone-on-tone paint to keep the low-key look alive and interesting. Soothing taupe is painted over the walls, then a paler, creamier version is painted on decorative crown molding. White paint on the doorway and wainscoting sharpens the look.

**More than mere words—one-of-kind design.** This bedroom, *above,* obviously is intended for twins. But lest the matching twin beds and mirror-image accessories keep you guessing, there's a can't-miss inscription painted on the wall to set the record straight. Homilies, or favorite sayings, or even family members' names can be painted onto walls to instantly customize the decor. Well-done, they are art—just as impactful as any framed painting or print. To get the correct typeface, enlarge letters from magazines, cut out on cardboard as stencils, sketch onto the walls, then paint.

**Use paint to float a tune and turn some heads.** The music is the message in this child's western room, *opposite.* And to make sure it hits home, the contrast is cranked up—fire-engine red walls, inscribed with a music staff and lyrics in black, and offset by a bright border of white crown molding. A star-studded stencil painted ceiling is the next best thing to camping out on the open range.

# FINISHES & MOTIFS

**Ivy-growing grace.** This bedroom's serene cottage character is created easily with paint, *opposite*. First, blank white walls are transformed with rich china blue. Then a touch of pattern is added by painting an ivy stencil that echoes the curves of the bed.

**Stencil around your furnishings.** One of the beauties of doing your own decorating is that you can make decisions in any order you choose. Instead of choosing a stencil pattern for the walls, then painting it uniformly into place, you can first arrange your furnishings—then stencil and paint around them, *above*. Note how the stenciling encircles the mirror above the mantel; between the windows, hand-painted swirls add polished, personal finishing touches.

**Tour decorator showhouses for inspiration and creative ideas.** Visit showhouses in your area for first-hand exposure to the newest looks in specialty paint finishes. If you're thinking of hiring an artist, check samples of his or her work in clients' homes or businesses. Most professionals have a portfolio with pictures. Show the artist what you like best, and go from there.

**Use specialty finishes sparingly.** One room or even a focal-point wall in one room creates interest. An entire house featuring different techniques or the

# TECHNIQUES

same technique in different colors can be jarring. However, if you choose a classic technique, such as sponging or soft ragging, and subtly blend colors, a specialty finish is an effective way to tie together rooms or adjoining spaces.

**Start with a sample.** Whether you are doing the finish yourself or hiring a painter, test on a sample board before tackling the walls. Then you can see how the technique looks and how it reflects natural and artificial light.

**Work out spacing.** For best results when you are painting on a pattern, plan and accurately pencil mark repeats before getting started.

# TECHNIQUES

**Take matters into your own hands.** Decorating with special paint techniques assumes personal meaning when family members take a hands-on approach. This clever treatment, *below,* lets children get into the act, decorating their walls with their own handprints. Blue rectangles frame the prints, the bulletin board, and the bed.

## ASSEMBLE THE RIGHT MATERIALS TO GET A GOOD START

■ Primer.

■ Paint.

■ Brown paper drop cloths for the floor; heavy plastic drop cloths for furniture.

■ Surfacing compound and knife to apply it, sandpaper, painter's tape, edger.

■ Metal paint pan, plastic liners, roller with threaded handle for extensions, sash and trim brushes. Most interior jobs call for a 7- or 9-inch roller frame. Use a long pole for the ceiling and short pole (2 feet long) for walls.

**There's more than one artist in the family.** Once you've embellished your child's bedroom with just the right peach paint on the walls and patterned paint treatments on the furnishings, *opposite,* step back and watch artistic skills bloom. A big blackboard, created with an easy-to-apply specialty paint, is just the canvas for unleashing creativity. To integrate it into the room, paint or stencil a whimsical border along its edges.

# TECHNIQUES

**Branch out from a corner.** This apple tree mural, *opposite*, leads the eye on a merry chase. Its branches cross the corner to span two walls. For a small room, limiting a mural to a single portion of the room like this enhances room size. For visual connection, the wall shelf and chest pulls are painted red to repeat the apple hue in the mural. **See page 46 for step-by-step how-to directions.**

**Made in the shade.** Although the artist used varying shades of green and brown for this shade-tree mural, *above,* you can paint a charming folk art version with one brown paint and one green and no shading or highlights. The paint colors used here are especially soft and subtle, for soothing pastoral comfort. **See page 46 for step-by-step how-to directions.**

**Make a primary statement.** Primary colors are among children's favorites, but they can be a little scary for parents wielding a paintbrush for the first time. To wash away fear, limit the primary colors to hand-painted accents that take up limited wall space, *opposite*. Purchase acrylic paints and several sizes of artist's brushes or small trim paintbrushes from the crafts store. To achieve the look of brushstrokes, don't use foam brushes.

**Draw your designs from a child's perspective.** You'll be amazed how much easier it is for you to paint—how much more confident and liberated you feel—once you've established your desired style as naive and childlike, as those shown here. The simpler the motifs, the better. The parents-to-be drew these designs freehand for a spontaneous look. If it makes you more comfortable, draw in soft pencil first, or use stencils for alphabet, numbers, and simple animals.

**Pencil in the border.** Measure and use pencil dots and ruled lines for a rough placement of the border, then paint on the color freehand.

**Think child-size, for scale and placement.** Call attention to your nifty artwork by placing it in your child's field of vision. Position people and animals near the floor, where they can be seen. Paint a house small so it's visually accessible—no bigger than a child's playhouse.

**Rag Rolling.** Use gloss or semigloss paint, which doesn't easily absorb. Apply a base coat of semigloss paint or thinned glaze; let it dry completely. Apply a second coat of a complementary color, using a roller or brush. Make sure the background color is several shades lighter than the paint you apply on top. Roll strips of clean cotton cloths, such as old T-shirts, for rags. Make three to five rolls before you start so you can work quickly. While the second coat is still wet, roll the fabric lightly over the surface from top to bottom, holding it at both ends. This partially removes the top color, exposing the base. If you haven't ragged, practice first. Change direction often. Discard the fabric roll once it becomes saturated.

**Do-It-Yourself Stencils.** You'll need clear acetate sheets (available at crafts stores), paper, masking tape, pencil, fine-point marker, stencil brushes, and a crafts knife. Draw your stencil pattern on paper. Tape an acetate sheet over your pattern and trace the area to be cut away with a fine-point marker. Use a crafts knife to cut out the stencil. Or purchase a stencil from crafts, hobby, or hardware stores. To paint, first tape the pattern in place. Dip the tip of a stencil brush into the paint, dabbing off excess on newsprint or on a clean cotton rag. Dab on paint to fill the cutout area, moving from the edges inward. The paint should leave a powdery finish. Let one stencil dry before overlayering another. When using more than one stencil, carefully remove the first stencil and let the paint dry. Align the guides on the second stencil, tape it in place, and paint.

# TECHNIQUES

**Sponging.** Paint a solid base coat of your color choice and let it dry overnight. Wear disposable plastic gloves instead of household rubber gloves, which leave fingerprint impressions. Change gloves as needed. Use a natural sea sponge for a soft, mottled appearance. Vary the sizes for interesting effects. To begin, wet the sponge with water and wring it out so paint will adhere. Pour a small amount of paint onto a foam plate, dip sponge in, and cover it with a small amount of paint. Blot excess. Cup the sponge in your hand and push lightly onto the surface. Practice first. Space sponged patches evenly, but change the sponge position for an irregular, mottled effect. Close, overlapping marks have a sleek look; widely spaced sponging with little or no overlap produces a casual appearance. Try spaced first, then fill in as need with additional sponging. A second or even a third blending color can be sponged over the base coat as desired.

**Combing.** Apply a base coat of flat paint. Let dry completely. Apply a complementary color of paint over the first layer. The top layer will darken the color of the undercoat somewhat. Comb the surface while the new layer is still wet, using a comb or other toothed instrument. A piece of heavy cardboard, cut into a comb, works well. Begin at the top of the wall—in a corner—and pull the comb through the paint or glaze. An extra hand is helpful for this step. While you brush on the coating, your partner follows and combs through the paint before it dries. Use long, clean strokes and wipe the comb clean after each run across or down the wall. Comb in the direction you prefer. The design does not require straight lines. Comb squiggly horizontal lines or bold vertical stripes if you like. The technique works well for limited surfaces, such as below a chair rail.

# QUICK TIPS ON MURALS

**Apple Tree Mural.** See page 38. **1. Protect the floor with drop cloths.** Make sure the room is well-ventilated and the windows are open. Paint the ceiling blue; let dry. Wear protective clothing, glasses, and a mask. Spray-paint hazy white clouds on the ceiling. Close the door so white paint doesn't blow into any other room. **2. Paint the walls.** Use your color choice; let dry. **3. Locate an image of a tree.** Trace the image onto tracing paper. Using an overhead projector, project the tracing-paper image as large as you wish on the wall. This image was enlarged to run over onto an adjacent wall. **4. Determine the size of the apple and leaf motifs.** Now cut out stencils. You'll need one stencil for the apple and one stencil each for the three sizes of leaves. **5. Lightly draw the projected tree image.** Trace it on the wall using a hard pencil. Don't press down or erase. If you project the image on two walls, be aware that the image will distort somewhat. Compensate by lengthening and shortening as needed when tracing the image on the wall. **6. Lightly draw the stencil motifs**. Stencil them onto the tree as directed in Step 5, overlapping the leaves and apples for a realistic look. **7. Use stencil crayons.** First stroke the crayon on heavy paper, then dab the stroked area with a clean, dry stencil brush. Hold the stencil to the wall; then, using a straight up-and-down motion of the brush, dab the color inside the stencil. Never color the wall directly with the crayon. **8. Create perspective with the stencil crayons.** First determine where light will strike the image, then color the shapes beginning with the darkest shades and moving to the lightest. For this apple tree, the right side of the trunk was heavily shaded, with white highlights sweeping down the trunk just left of center. The round shape is further suggested with narrow but heavy shading on the left side of the trunk. To ground the tree, create dark shading where roots spread. Also add dark shading at crevices where the limbs begin and spread. To give dimension to the apples, use dark shading at the outer edges; add white highlights to create a play of sunlight and to emphasize the dips for the stems. Shade the leaves darker at the outer edges and create larger areas of highlighting on leaves in the center of the tree.

**Mural Magic.** See page 39. **1. Sketch designs on paper.** Keep the sketch simple, focusing on the main features: the trunk, branches, and large blocks of leaves. **2. Use #5 or #6 pencil.** Lightly sketch the design on the wall. See Step 5 of Apple Tree Mural for instructions. **3. Practice painting on scrap plywood or cardboard.** This will help to perfect your technique. Work with watered-down acrylics and paint a small section of the trunk, branch, and leaves at one time, as directed below. **4. Water down the darkest shade.** This will turn the brown paint to the consistency of wall paint. Paint the darkest areas of the trunk and branches first, referring to Step 8 of the Apple Tree Mural. Apply at least two more shades of brown, each lighter than the preceding one, to suggest perspective and roundness. For the leaves, use dampened natural sponges to dab on three shades of green. Sponge the wall with the darkest shade first and finish with the lightest on top. Don't let the paint dry between colors; blend paint between colors for a subtle, natural appearance. Add highlights by sponging on and blending in dabs of pale yellow.